The Weight of Resolve

Gerald Locke

The Weight of Resolve

Published by Locke Publishing

ISBN: 978-1-972281-21-5

Cover and interior design: Gerald Locke
Printed in the United States of America
Discover more books by Gerald Locke:
GeraldLocke.com
Follow for updates and new releases:
TikTok: @geraldlockeauthor
Facebook: Gerald Locke – Author

Contents

Introduction

These poems span from 1999 to 2017. What begins as instinct evolves into structure—revealing a consistent thematic core refined over time: constraint, pressure, inevitability, and consequence.

Section I — The Fracture

$(2^{008-2011)}$

Madness

October 2017
Voices scream and shrill within
Grotesque images, unspeakable thoughts
Demanding crimson atonement
Another victim to satiate the hunger

Subservient to malicious desires
Rivulets descend from metallic kisses
Like dew on a morning flower
Creating my serrated lover's chef-d'oeuvre

Riddle Me This

June 2016
His shadow is always upon you
A presence at the edge of your thoughts
Like a hidden voice within your mind

A whisper that can bring an end to pain
Like a lover's tender kiss
Ever present in your darkest thoughts

A guide to see you through the abyss
A friend or foe by circumstance

Always abiding, awaiting his moment
Lunging forward when it is time
To take his due inheritance

Psicose

August 2013

Anxious, tangled, infuriated
Crimson envelopes darkness
Reverberating
Engaging

Another breath
Whispers within

Ceaseless warring
Leave me alone
Visions or veracity
Endless voices

Respite a ceaseless pursuit

The Struggle Within

October 2008

The war rages within my soul
Evil spreading throughout
Thoughts of malice intensify
As my mind loses control
My heart becomes black
My blood courses cold
I am infatuated with thirst
A craving for flesh and pain
Brazen thoughts of slaughter
Are vexatious as I struggle
Powerless to prevail
Reluctant to concede
I envy death's reprieve

Shadow of Darkness

October 2008

Lost within the dark forest of my mind
The shadows overcoming my emotions
There is no escape

Unable to fight
Unable to continue
Unable to persevere

I surrender my soul to the darkness
The dark shadows begin their infiltration
I still have no peace

Trapped Inside My Fears

October 2008

Behind the frame
My fears are kept
Unable to escape
A prisoner
Within my flesh

The Pit of Sorrow

May 2011

Memories past
Dreams shattered
Time moves on
Days into years
What once I knew
Now lost in tears
A waking nightmare
Tormenting my soul
Unable to escape
Closing in around me
Drowning in darkness
Unable to breathe
No end in sight
Consumed by grief
Endless plight
Sorrow swells
Numbing pain
Cannot rest

Forever Lost

October 2008

 Lying upon the shores of insanity
Stripped bare of my freedom
The doorway to my innocence
Forever closed behind me
I remain lifeless and
Eternally lost in torment
Without reprieve

Section II — The Hunger

$(2^{013)}$

Σαίμονας εσωτερικής

September 2013

    Voices shroud my thoughts
Powerless to escape
Louder they become
Endless chattering

Just one more

Insatiable appetite
I can taste their desire
A putrid flavor
There is no compromise

Must have more

Scent of fear arousing
Voices dominate
She sleeps in innocence
Symphonic heartbeat

She will suffice

Confidence builds
Salivate with anticipation
Steel dancing across her throat
Sweet crimson serenade

Silence at last

Unrelenting Appetite

October 2013
Crimson flows with joyful bliss
A symphony of screams
Fears scent salivates
Cadavers strung along my rack
Each morsel a delectable delight
Massacre's never adequate

Cadaverous Ecstasies

June 2016

Macabre thoughts sing tender lullabies
Entrapped inside my frigid mind
Passionately embraced deafening screams
Everlasting carnage lovingly caresses
Beautiful massacres vividly unfold
Within entombed insanity

Elated Asphyxiation

June 2016

> Errant shadows shrewd and secure
Saturate his tightened esophagus
Like sunshine soaks the effervescent sea

Feverish and fervent endeavors
Are intoxicated with utter euphoric delight

Pulsated pressure palpates
Beneath my forceful grasp
As life ebbs away like an ocean's tide

Joy of the Hunt

October 2013
      Fear streams from your pores
Scent engulfing my nostrils
Enticing my senses
Taunting my desires
The hunt is always salivating
Anticipation heightens the thrill
I can taste your demise
A sweet delicacy
Each scream orgasmic
Terror is always savory

True Love

October 2013
  Death's adoration my liberation
Tears and crimson ebbing
A beautiful symphony
Only death can understand

Anticipation of our convening
Coursing through my veins
Unrelenting hunger
Death my one true love

Crimson Malice

O ctober 2008
        Vivid scenes envelope my thoughts
Surrounding his inevitable demise
With haste I must determine his fate
His breathing corpse is firmly bound
His awakening is ever close
My decision is now at hand
His torment will become legend
On the lips who speak his name
Ne'er before has this town known
The horrors I will bring
He is honored as my victim
His death will be renowned
Visions of his crimson blood
Will be etched in innocent minds
Terror will devour all hope
As his bloodshed devours my rage
The scent burning flesh
Engulfing my nostrils
Quickening my thoughts
As flames lick against his skin
His screams are the music

That fills my soul with joy
The flames only a taste
Of the torment to follow
His skin charred and still he breathes
Unable to escape his living hell
Piece by piece I shred his skin
His crimson blood flowing
Heart racing beneath his ribs
Nerves glimmering against his spine
Tears of blood shower his cheeks
His prayer for release not answered
My torment is not complete
A final laugh is all he sees
As I thrust my hand into his chest
His beating heart within my grasp
A twist, a scream, my final trophy

Hungers Abomination

January 2013
    Feasting children
Enraged depravity
Hatred slowly consuming
Maternal bond
Maternal body
Severed and savored
Ebbing decreases
Violent urges
Father's final plea

Who's next

Kill the Bastard

2009

Knowledge of his deeds
Innocence shattered
Living a lie
Lost

Tomorrow brings hope
His death imminent
Eternal damnation

Blood boils in his veins
Another gasp is heard
Silence soon follows
Tomorrow brings peace
A new day begins
Remorse not an option
Death his only friend

Emotional Abyss

October 2008

    Even as you are strung above
Unable to fathom my intentions
I continue to envy you
Envy your ability to know emotions
To understand what they are
To feel hate, love, sorrow, grief
Something I could never do

Fear gleaming from your eyes
Do you not understand
Can you not comprehend
I, too, must feel emotion
I must know what it is to feel
I only know hunger and thirst
Only death and torment satisfy

In your death I will know joy
As your blood leisurely pours
I will come to know ecstasy
You will have peace through me
No longer will you suffer

Your pains will become my pleasure
Your sorrow will be my delight

The first slit on your chest
Pure, unadulterated bliss
As I begin tearing apart your flesh
I now understand what joy is
Your screams such sweet music
My knife the instrument
Alas, emotion envelopes my soul

This is the rush I desire
To watch your fleeting soul
Your heart beating slowly
Like that of an instrument
Unable to keep in tempo
The fear escaping your eyes
Only a prayer for release

Your blood, so sweet and warm
I can taste it on my lips
Such a rush of emotions
Joy, Ecstasy, Pleasure, Delight
Saturated with your blood
Your heart has stopped beating
Again, I stand emotionless

Section III — The System

$(2^{013-2017})$

Welcome to the Garden

October 2013

Bloody Mary, quite contrary,
How does your graveyard grow?
Where horrors dwell with putrid smells
And corpses strewn in rows

Vile scenes engulf my vision
Your garden's full of gore
Intestines strewn across the graves
Bowels and limbs galore

Aorta veins placed on headstones
Organs skewered on stakes
Spines still shimmer along the paths
Worms feasting like the plague

Mourning sounds inundate the air
Putrid essence abounds
Hands reaching from beneath the graves
Your victim's souls still bound

Welcome to the Party

October 2013

Darkness concealed behind my smiles
Voices within commanding more
Intense desire for eternal life
Ingesting flesh to lengthen mine
Their vitality must become my own

A dinner party full of guests
They dance and dine throughout the night
Each bite, each sip, a subterfuge
Their deaths a necessity
Their life force required
Eternally paralyzed as poison sets in

One by one each take their place
My cellar fills with new souls
Blood wine now replenished
With each swallow my life extended
Never enough to satisfy
Eternal life my indomitable desire

Cadaver Revenge

May 2016

Expression of dread upon her face
A mortal thrust against the blade
Crimson rivulets adorning her dress
Life's grasp upon her finally fades

Enthralling satisfaction of another kill
Blissful rest I can endure
The voices squelched for the eve
Her body buried beneath the shore

My tools replaced and respite found
Another prolific night
I lay upon my satin sheets
As slumber takes its rite

Her crimson eyes engulf my slumber
Her whispers haunt my dream
"I can't sleep" she repeats
And moves in place beside me

Paralyzed I am unable to breathe

Her hand reaches into my chest
Endless grasp on my beating heart
Unbearable pain, torment, unrest

I feel my heart crush within her hand
I am aghast at this event
I put her to rest beneath the shore
She should be long stagnant
I thrust awake unable to breath
My mind a jumbled mess
My life is ebbing beneath the sheets
And I am left clenching a crimson dress

Insanity's Wilderness

August 2013
    Within my wilderness escape is an illusion
Only doorway raven oversees
Only one exit – your death
Run where you can, hide where you must
Your imminent expiration is assured demise

Glimpse your future within my forest
Piles of festering organs and flesh
Corpses strewn along trees
Sweet smell of decay
Slow tortured souls
Such delectable sights

Hairs bristling behind your neck
Ragged breathing and racing heart
Whispers in your ear
Succulent taste of fear
Ahead you stumble

Don't sleep too long
You'll miss your own death

Slowly at first you awaken
Knife cutting through your flesh
Blood flows effortlessly as raven begins his feast
Securely fastened along multiple limbs
Unable to escape excruciating pain

Screams only bring me pleasure
Lungs behind rib cage expand as heart quickens
Spine glows with an eerie light
Intestines extruding like noodles
Knife moves swiftly with ease and precision
Skin removed, torso exposed

Breaths more shallow as screams diminish
Time to remove ribs one by one
What joyous sounds as ribs give way
Snacks for my wilderness friends
Life still clings, heart still beats

Moving lower to your thighs
Removing mouthwatering pieces

With a saw your brains exposed
Tiny morsels are Raven's delicacies
A piece sliced off and force fed
Final thrust through the heart
Surging pleasure within

Dinner is served

The Evil Side of OZ

September 2008

    The mirror begins to shimmer
Like the ripples in a lake
My room turns cold as winter
As the walls begin to quake

The storm's wrath comes gravely near
And my reflection takes new shape
The window shatters strong and fierce
As I collapse upon my face

I awaken with such fright
Encircled by small men
They seem to quiver at the sight
Of such a large woman

Thier chants are dark and horrid
And it rings within my ears
About the death so morbid
Of their chief for many years

How a house fell from the sky

And landed on his head
How when they came to look inside
They found their chief was dead

Amidst all of their commotion
A beast had entered in
They scattered at the notion
Of being its next victim

This gave me just one chance
Out the window I did dart
I turned my head for one last glance
To see the beast tear them apart

My heart sunk within my chest
And I stopped to take a breath
Something then just touched my dress
And scared me half to death

A scarecrow abreast his post
Had laid his hands on me
At first I thought it was a ghost
Then he asked to be set free

Frightened I pulled the nails
That held him to his post
He fell upon the ground
Then staggered to his toes

He thanked me for his freedom
Then right before my eyes
He grabbed my throat for fun
And tried to take my life

I was about to pass out
When a man made out of tin
Came charging forth with a shout
And did the scarecrow in

He asked for my forgiveness
As he pulled me to my feet
He said he had a weakness
For violence in his streets

I told him of my story
And he gave me an evil grin
Said I need not to worry
If I just stay with him

We hurried upon the bricks
As we passed by many trees
Then appeared an ugly witch
And brought us to our knees

The trees began their laughter
As the man of tin did rust
Her spell became much quicker
As the man was now but dust

She said that I would never
Reach the end of this long path
I would be stuck here forever
And she would see to that

She gave me an evil glance
Then up in smoke she flew
The forest now took its chance
Its fruit at me they threw

I hurried through the forest
When a lion crossed my path
Hungry and on his quest
I was certain to see his wrath

He began to lunge towards me
Hunger was in his eyes
He gave a roar to bared his teeth
Then I noticed he was blind

I stood in simple stillness
And did not make a sound
He kept looking for a scent
But one could not be found

He lingered along his way
And some time I let pass by
I did not want to make the prey
Return to take a bite

I came upon my house again
Fearful I now became
Circles I must have traveled in
Was this some kind of game

All the men were butchered
The beast had long departed
The men had not endured
This is where it all had started

I entered through to front
And took a glance around
I truly became stunned

To find my mirror was still sound

I stood it upon the boards
And gazed upon the glass
What I saw was horrid
My reflection did not look back

I did not see any debris
As if nothing had gone awry
An image of what looked like me
Was on the bed nearby

I beat hard upon the glass
And my image gave a smile
My fears quickly amassed
As my image became hostile

She came to the glass with haste
An evil laugh filled the air
"Now my life you have a taste"
"You are going nowhere"

Section IV — The Outcome

$(1^{999-2016})$

Evil Incarnate

June 2011

Insidious laughter
You clutch my heart
Punctured with your deceit
Blood pools at your feet

Vengeance is Mine

October 2008

    Last night I entered into his demented chapel
In search for my Charlotte's dear priest
Vague memories of her laughter haunt my thoughts
Inescapable hunger for vengeance engulfing my soul
Now the time of reckoning is at hand
Going forth to put an end to his savagery

The chapel doors stand just before me
Hell waiting on the other side
Righteous justice is just moments away
Openly he greets my entrance
Unaware he is to be my next victim
Gravely mistaken me as one of his flock
His voice so confident and clear

Hunger fills the depths of my soul
Even as I approach her murderer
Little suspicion of his own fate
Like a fly being drawn to the web

In velvet robes he greets me

So child, what can I do for you?

Heaven, father, does not await you
Another fate has been chosen
Victims demand for your punishment
I am here to fulfill their commands
Now your chapel becomes your prison
God can not help you

A needle pierced into his neck
Now you will know true evil

Underneath the glimmering light of the moon
Not able to escape
Strange, father, that I would choose your chamber?
After all this is where you took her life
Time is of no concern for me
I have all night to ensure your suffering
Satisfaction will be mine
For the death of my sweet Charlotte
I will make you pay
A tribute to her unholy grave
Because she trusted you
Loved you like a father
Even till the night you stole her away

Have you no remorse for your actions
Under the name of God you take innocence
No mercy for the children you prey
Great pleasure you take in their suffering
Empowering yourself through their pain
Renouncing your faith with each drop of blood

Fate, it seems, has brought us together

Only those who are worthy do I prey upon
Rather demented souls that I deliver

Tonight you become honored as my victim
On this night you shall be redeemed
Repentance in blood you shall provide tonight
Torture is but sanctification before deliverance
Under this hallowed roof your blood will run
Rivers of repentance for you deeds
Even as I become your deliverer

A chance for you to redeem yourself
Now let's begin your deliverance
Deeply I slice into his ribs

Demonic thoughts enveloping my mind
Every inch bringing pleasure
Atonement for his deeds
Thrashing in his chains he screams
Hoping to escape

Tearing apart his ribs I see
His heart racing as the blood flows
And his lungs filling deeply
Trying to withstand the pain

Even now my hunger grows
Vainly seeking satisfaction
Enveloping my every thought
Numbing my senses

Slowly I rip through his abdomen
Another scream echoes from his throat
Terrible his pain must be

Another reason to continue
No mercy can be shown

His heart begins to slow
I know his time is limited
My vengeance is at hand
Swiftly I must complete the deed
Even now he gasps for air
Life drains unhurriedly from his corpse
Faint screams still echoing

With a clenched fist I grab within
Out pours his intestines
Unwilling to relinquish his soul
Life still struggling to remain
Death is inevitable

Even now as his life begins to fade
New blood flowing on the floor
Victory is mine
Your death is my beginning

Revenge

1^{999} The body hangs by hands and feet
Freshly skinned exposing meat
With their knives they start to cut
As if the skin was not enough
The meat comes off in screams and cries
For the man has not yet died
Now with a saw the ribs are cut
Exposing all his bloody guts
The lungs still move; the man still breathes
They take a bat and break his knees
The bones are shattered one by one
All the while men laugh in fun
They punch his lung with a knife
Hoping that they'll take his life
He still breathes but violently
As the hole flaps in the breeze
His heart hangs low held on by veins
Trying its best to beat again
Behind his heart and lungs and so
They can see his spines nerves glow
Hanging by a group of nerves

Are his eyes down in the dirt
Although the man still tries to breathe
They stab his heart to set him free

Reborn

June 2016

   Broken bones and endless bruises
   Heart torn asunder
   Opinions brushed aside
   Like dust on a windowsill

   He said, "I love you"
   "I'm sorry" every time
   Each slap a reminder
   Of how much I hated myself

   Will was bent
   Never broken
   Leaving was as easy
   As walking barefoot across broken glass

   Crimson footprints can't stop me
   They only strengthen me

Freedom From You
   October 2008

My pain has now ceased
Your corpse can speak no deceptions
Lying beside me
Relief fills my soul
The pain you caused has ended
In your death I'm whole
Free from your torments
Freed from your brutality
My heart can now rest
Relief and reprieve
Your death becomes my rebirth
Your silence sublime
I cast one last glance
Your endless rest brings me peace
At last I am free

Section V — The Anchor

$$(2^{008})$$

Before the Final Poem

This collection was written after a period of my life defined by abuse.

During that time, I wrote—but not what you find here. My writing took the form of fiction, of distance, of anything that allowed separation from what was happening. Those works served their purpose, but they are not part of this book.

The poems in this collection came later.

They were written after the abuse ended. After the person responsible was no longer in my life. What remains in these pages is not a direct record of those events, but something shaped by what followed them—how pressure lingers, how it restructures thought, how it leaves behind patterns that do not simply disappear.

The final piece is different.

It stands apart from the rest of the collection in its proximity to truth. Not in detail, but in origin. It is the closest this book comes to the source of what shaped everything around it.

It is placed last for that reason.

Everything before it exists within structure—progression, escalation, consequence. The final piece does not follow that same containment. It does not need to.

It remains.

Why Me?

October 2008
　　A secret that haunts my waking dreams
Eroding away at my conscience
My innocence taken
My emotions grown cold
Unable to comprehend
Why Me?

I was only a child
An innocent soul still seeking truth
My trust was wrongfully placed
An evil deed ensued

Without cause or refrain
Violated in the most despicable way
Unable to make a sound
Could not stop him
What terrible pain
Why Me?

Fearing to go to bed
Knowing the terror that awaited

A boys dreams now nightmares
Never ending torment

What wrongs did I do
To deserve such degradation
Enduring such pain
Unable to scream
Not knowing its end
Why Me?

I would pray for death
Every time he entered me
Pushing deeper inside
Such intolerable pain

I could not tell a soul
Great embarrassment and fear
I would be at fault
I should have stopped him
But how could I?
Why Me?

Unconceivable acts
Forced upon my innocence
Such a terrible taste
Constantly gagging

Nightmares still ensue
Emotions almost empty
My innocence was stolen
My childhood destroyed
Such horrible memories
Why Me?

Why Me?

Why Me?

Thank You for Reading

Your time means everything.

If this story resonated with you, please consider leaving a brief review on Amazon.

Even a single sentence helps new readers discover my work.

Explore More Books by Gerald Locke

For a complete list of published works—including horror, epic fantasy, cosmic fantasy, modern hidden-magic, and stand-alones—visit:

GeraldLocke.com

You'll find:

- full book catalog
- reading guides
- future releases
- world lore
- author updates

Connect With the Author

For book trailers, updates, and behind-the-scenes content:

TikTok: **@geraldlockeauthor**

Facebook: **Gerald Locke – Author**

Website: **GeraldLocke.com**

Thank You for Supporting Independent Fiction
Your curiosity keeps these worlds alive.
I hope we cross paths again in the next story.